In a community, some things continue and some things change.

SCHOLASTIC

LITERACY PLACE®

Copyright acknowledgments and credits appear on page 136, which constitutes an extension of this copyright page.

Copyright © 1996 by Scholastic Inc.   All rights reserved.   Printed in the U.S.A.
                                              ISBN 0-590-49160-1

            6 7 8 9 10   24   02 01 00

Visit
a Community Garden

In a community, some things continue and some things change.

That's the Spirit!

A community improves through the contributions of individuals.

Interested in joining...
Linden Heights Neighborhood Garden?
Find out how...
Come to a garden planning meeting

New Horizons

A community grows through the contributions of newcomers.

Family Biscuits

2 cups all-purpose flour
1 tablespoon baking powder
½ teaspoon salt
⅓ cup shortening
¾ cup milk

1. Heat oven to 425°F.

Keepsakes

A community is strengthened by preserving landmarks and traditions.

Trade Books

The following books accompany this *Community Quilt* SourceBook.

AWARD WINNING Author

City Green

by DyAnne DiSalvo-Ryan

AWARD WINNING Book

Cloudy With a Chance of Meatballs

by Judi Barrett
illustrated by
Ron Barrett

AWARD WINNING Author

Lily and Miss Liberty

by Carla
Stevens
illustrated by
Deborah Kogan
Ray

AWARD WINNING Book

Samuel's Choice

by Richard
Berleth
illustrated by
James Watling

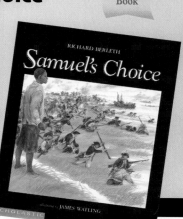

A community improves through the contributions of individuals.

That's the Spirit!

Join Peter Stuyvesant as he cleans up old New York. Then discover how present-day Pittsburgh fought pollution—and won.

Find out how a dream helps a litterbug change his ways.

Dig into Dayton, Ohio's community gardens with Lorka Muñoz.

WORKSHOP 1

Create a public-service poster for your community.

Interested in joining...
Linden Heights Neighborhood Garden?
Find out how...
Come to a garden planning meeting
Thursday, July 6
St. Anthony School Cafeteria
6:30 - 7:00 p.m.

9

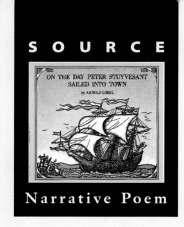

On The Day Peter Stuyvesant Sailed Into Town

by ARNOLD LOBEL

On the day Peter Stuyvesant sailed into town
All the people came running to greet him.
They shot off a cannon and waited in line
So that every last Dutchman could meet him.

11

"My friends," Peter said, "it is nice to be here
For my voyage was really a long one.
I will rule this new land with a very firm hand,
And my government will be a strong one.
Yes, my government will be a strong one."

Peter Stuyvesant stood with a leg made of wood,
And he said, "There is no time to talk now.
It's a very fine day, this eleventh of May,
So I think I will go for a walk now."

And into New Amsterdam Peter did go
To see all there was to be seen.
But he soon wore a frown as he walked up and down—
He discovered that nothing was clean.

The governor slipped in the mud and the mire,
And he said, "Things are not at all well here.
I am standing in garbage right up to my knees,
And the air has a very bad smell here.
Yes, the air has a very bad smell here."

"All the houses in town are in need of repair,"
Peter shouted. "I loudly decry it!
This whole dirty place is a total disgrace.
Good Dutchmen, we must beautify it!"

But the folk of the town went on smoking their pipes,
And they said, "It is best to ignore him.
There will soon come a day he will be on his way
Like the men who have governed before him."

From Broadway to Wall Street old Stuyvesant stormed;
With a tap and a step he kept walking,
While some chickens and ducks made a nest in his hat
And some geese on the path made a squawking.
Yes, those geese on the path made a squawking.

Then a goat from behind, in a manner unkind,
Gave Peter a push on his seat.
A cow licked his nose and some pigs chewed his toes
As poor Stuyvesant sat in the street.

"This New World is a mess!" Peter cried in distress.
"These animals need gates and fences.
Take these birds to a cage!" Peter shouted in rage.
"Oh, good Dutchmen, let's come to our senses!"

As his voice rocked the ground with a great, booming sound,
Like a sky filled with thunder and lightning,
Those good Dutchmen did shake—they cried, "Make no mistake,
This man's temper is really quite frightening!"

While the citizens stood in a trembling group
Peter cried, "Here is my proclamation.
All you men and you maids, get your brooms and your spades.
We must work now without hesitation!
Yes, let's work now without hesitation!"

So they put up new buildings all sturdy and strong,
And they cleaned all the rubbish away.
They mended the fences and paved many streets
From the top of the town to the bay.

They filled up the holes in the walls of the fort,
For the colony needed protection.
And the people agreed they were clever to heed
Peter Stuyvesant's careful direction.

Some ten or twelve summers had come and had gone
As they worked on the east and the west side.
Things were going so well it was soon hard to tell
Which half of that town was the best side.

"My children," said Peter, "we've worked very hard,
And I think we deserve relaxation.
I feel in the mood for some fun and some food.
Let us have a big Dutch celebration!
Yes, it's time for a big celebration!"

Each New Amsterdam nose sniffed the smells that arose
In delicious fat clouds to the air.
How they gave such delight to each Dutch appetite,
All those good things to eat everywhere.

Someone asked, "Will this town stay as small as it is?"
Well, of course, there was no way of knowing,
So they danced until evening all dizzy and gay
And went home as the darkness was growing.

That night Peter Stuyvesant heard a strange sound
Underneath a round moon brightly gleaming.
It swept past his door, a great tumble and roar,
But old Stuyvesant knew he was dreaming.

Yes, Peter Stuyvesant knew he was dreaming.

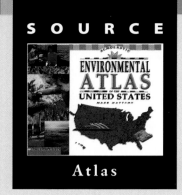
from
Scholastic Environmental Atlas
of the United States

How Pittsburgh

by Mark Mattson

Here is what Pittsburgh looked like when its steel mills were thriving, and how it looks today. Industry in the cities around the Great Lakes— especially steel-works—had declined so much by the 1980s that the area was often described as the Rust Belt.

Cleaned Up

Pittsburgh became an industrial, steel-making giant about 100 years ago. Three major rivers—the Monongahela, the Ohio, and the Allegheny—meet in this western Pennsylvania city. These rivers were used to move iron ore and coal into Pittsburgh's furnaces, and to move finished steel out.

Eventually, the rivers became polluted and started flooding. Belching smokestacks dirtied the air. Huge heaps of slag, the waste from making steel, blemished the earth.

First Clean-up. In the 1950s, industrialists and political leaders joined together to clean up the city. They passed anti-smoke laws to clean up the air. They created locks and dams to tame the rivers. They replaced industrial slums with parks, plazas, and modern buildings.

By the 1970s, Pittsburgh's steel factories were outdated, and the steel industry was failing. As jobs were lost, neighborhoods crumbled.

Good Place to Live. City leaders again joined together to bring in clean industries that use technologies such as biomedicine, robotics, and software to create new jobs. In 1985, Pittsburgh was named America's most livable city. Today, people can even fish in the Monongahela.

Pittsburgh's Three Rivers

JUST A DREAM
BY CHRIS VAN ALLSBURG

As usual, Walter stopped at the bakery on his way home
from school. He bought one large jelly-filled doughnut.
He took the pastry from its bag, eating quickly as he
walked along. He licked the red jelly from his fingers.
Then he crumpled up the empty bag and threw it at a
fire hydrant.

At home Walter saw Rose, the little girl next door, watering a tree that had just been planted. "It's my birthday present," she said proudly. Walter couldn't understand why anyone would want a tree for a present. His own birthday was just a few days away, "And I'm not getting some dumb plant," he told Rose.

After dinner Walter took out the trash. Three cans stood next to the garage. One was for bottles, one for cans, and one for everything else. As usual, Walter dumped everything into one can. He was too busy to sort through garbage, especially when there was something good on television.

The show that Walter was so eager to watch was about a boy who lived in the future. The boy flew around in a tiny airplane that he parked on the roof of his house. He had a robot and a small machine that could make any kind of food with the push of a button.

Walter went to bed wishing he lived in the future. He couldn't wait to have his own tiny plane, a robot to take out the trash, and a machine that could make jelly doughnuts by the thousands. When he fell asleep, his wish came true. That night Walter's bed traveled to . . .

the future.

Walter woke up in the middle of a huge dump. A bulldozer was pushing a heap of bulging trash bags toward him. "Stop!" he yelled.

The man driving the bulldozer put his machine in neutral. "Oh, sorry," he said. "Didn't see you."

Walter looked at the distant mountains of trash and saw half-buried houses. "Do people live here?" he asked.

"Not anymore," answered the man.

A few feet from the bed was a rusty old street sign that read FLORAL AVENUE. "Oh no," gasped Walter. He lived on Floral Avenue.

The driver revved up his bulldozer. "Well," he shouted, "back to work!"

Walter pulled the covers over his head. This can't be the future, he thought. I'm sure it's just a dream. He went back to sleep.

But not for long . . .

Walter peered over the edge of his bed, which was caught in the branches of a tall tree. Down below, he could see two men carrying a large saw. "Hello!" Walter yelled out.

"Hello to you!" they shouted back.

"You aren't going to cut down this tree, are you?" Walter asked.

But the woodcutters didn't answer. They took off their jackets, rolled up their sleeves, and got to work. Back and forth they pushed the saw, slicing through the trunk of Walter's tree. "You must need this tree for something important," Walter called down.

"Oh yes," they said, "very important." Then Walter noticed lettering on the woodcutters' jackets. He could just make out the words: QUALITY TOOTHPICK COMPANY. Walter sighed and slid back under the blankets.

Until . . .

Walter couldn't stop coughing. His bed was balanced on the rim of a giant smokestack. The air was filled with smoke that burned his throat and made his eyes itch. All around him, dozens of smokestacks belched thick clouds of hot, foul smoke. A workman climbed one of the stacks.

"What is this place?" Walter called out.

"This is the Maximum Strength Medicine Factory," the man answered.

"Gosh," said Walter, looking at all the smoke, "what kind of medicine do they make here?"

"Wonderful medicine," the workman replied, "for burning throats and itchy eyes."

Walter started coughing again.

"I can get you some," the man offered.

"No thanks," said Walter. He buried his head in his pillow and, when his coughing stopped, fell asleep.

But then . . .

Snowflakes fell on Walter. He was high in the mountains.
A group of people wearing snowshoes and long fur coats
hiked past his bed.

"Where are you going?" Walter asked.

"To the hotel," one of them replied.

Walter turned around and saw an enormous building.
A sign on it read HOTEL EVEREST. "Is that hotel," asked
Walter, "on the top of Mount Everest?"

"Yes," said one of the hikers. "Isn't it beautiful?"

"Well," Walter began. But the group didn't wait for
his answer. They waved goodbye and marched away.
Walter stared at the flashing yellow sign, then crawled
back beneath his sheets.

But there was more to see . . .

Walter's hand was wet and cold. When he opened his eyes, he found himself floating on the open sea, drifting toward a fishing boat. The men on the boat were laughing and dancing.

"Ship ahoy!" Walter shouted.

The fishermen waved to him.

"What's the celebration for?" he asked.

"We've just caught a fish," one of them yelled back. "Our second one this week!" They held up their small fish for Walter to see.

"Aren't you supposed to throw the little ones back?" Walter asked.

But the fishermen didn't hear him. They were busy singing and dancing.

Walter turned away. Soon the rocking of the bed put him to sleep.

But only for a moment . . .

A loud, shrieking horn nearly lifted Walter off his mattress. He jumped up. There were cars and trucks all around him, horns honking loudly, creeping along inch by inch. Every driver had a car phone in one hand and a big cup of coffee in the other. When the traffic stopped completely, the honking grew even louder. Walter could not get back to sleep.

Hours passed, and he wondered if he'd be stuck on this highway forever. He pulled his pillow tightly around his head. This can't be the future, he thought. Where are the tiny airplanes, the robots? The honking continued into the night, until finally, one by one, the cars became quiet as their drivers, and Walter, went to sleep.

But his bed traveled on . . .

Walter looked up. A horse stood right over his bed, staring directly at him. In the saddle was a woman wearing cowboy clothes. "My horse likes you," she said.

"Good," replied Walter, who wondered where he'd ended up this time. All he could see was a dull yellow haze.

"Son," the woman told him, spreading her arms in front of her, "this is the mighty Grand Canyon."

Walter gazed into the foggy distance.

"Of course," she went on, "with all this smog, nobody's gotten a good look at it for years." The woman offered to sell Walter some postcards that showed the canyon in the old days. "They're real pretty," she said.

But he couldn't look. It's just a dream, he told himself. I know I'll wake up soon, back in my room.

But he didn't . . .

Walter looked out from under his sheets. His bed was flying through the night sky. A flock of ducks passed overhead. One of them landed on the bed, and to Walter's surprise, he began to speak. "I hope you don't mind," the bird said, "if I take a short rest here." The ducks had been flying for days, looking for the pond where they had always stopped to eat.

"I'm sure it's down there somewhere," Walter said, though he suspected something awful might have happened. After a while the duck waddled to the edge of the bed, took a deep breath, and flew off. "Good luck," Walter called to him. Then he pulled the blanket over his head. "It's just a dream," he whispered, and wondered if it would ever end.

Then finally . . .

Walter's bed returned to the present. He was safe in his room again, but he felt terrible. The future he'd seen was not what he'd expected. Robots and little airplanes didn't seem very important now. He looked out his window at the trees and lawns in the early morning light, then jumped out of bed.

He ran outside and down the block, still in his pajamas. He found the empty jelly doughnut bag he'd thrown at the fire hydrant the day before. Then Walter went back home and, before the sun came up, sorted all the trash by the garage.

A few days later, on Walter's birthday, all his friends came
over for cake and ice cream. They loved his new toys: the
laser gun set, electric yo-yo, and inflatable dinosaurs. "My
best present," Walter told them, "is outside." Then he
showed them the gift that he'd picked out that
morning—a tree.

After the party, Walter and his dad planted the birthday present. When he went to bed, Walter looked out his window. He could see his tree and the tree Rose had planted on her birthday. He liked the way they looked, side by side. Then he went to sleep, but not for long, because that night Walter's bed took him away again.

When Walter woke up, his bed was standing in the shade of two tall trees. The sky was blue. Laundry hanging from a clothesline flapped in the breeze. A man pushed an old motorless lawnmower. This isn't the future, Walter thought. It's the past.

"Good morning," the man said. "You've found a nice place to sleep."

"Yes, I have," Walter agreed. There was something very peaceful about the huge trees next to his bed.

The man looked up at the rustling leaves. "My great-grandmother planted one of these trees," he said, "when she was a little girl."

Walter looked up at the leaves too, and realized where his bed had taken him. This was the future, after all, a different kind of future. There were still no robots or tiny airplanes. There weren't even any clothes dryers or gas-powered lawn mowers. Walter lay back and smiled. "I like it here," he told the man, then drifted off to sleep in the shade of the two giant trees—the trees he and Rose had planted so many years ago.

Lorka Muñoz

Grow With Us
Community Garden

·KIDS' PLOTS AVAILABLE·

A GROW WITH YOUR NEIGHBOR'S GARDEN
of the Wegerzyn Horticultural Center
with the Support of the
City of Dayton's
Department of Planning

Community Garden Director

Learn why *community gardens* are here to stay.

Take an empty city lot filled with rusty cans, plastic bottles, and weeds. Add a group of hard-working people, some flower and vegetable seeds, and a few trees. What do you have? "A community garden," says Lorka Muñoz with a big smile.

PROFILE

Name: Lorka Muñoz

Job: community garden director

Born: New York City

What *lorka* means: "Flower" in Russian. With a different spelling, it is also the last name of a famous Spanish poet.

Hobby: fixing up old houses

Most unusual garden you have seen: A kids' garden in Denver, Colorado. The kids used junk to make scarecrows.

Community projects you did as a kid: planting trees

47

ALL ABOUT
Lorka Muñoz

Here's what Lorka Muñoz *has to say about* **starting a community garden.**

Lorka Muñoz works for an organization in Dayton, Ohio, called Grow With Your Neighbors (GWYN). She helps people all over the city turn empty lots into neighborhood green spots.

"A community garden usually starts with one or two people who have found a place for a garden," says Muñoz. "The first thing I do is meet with them and describe how GWYN can help. Then they start organizing other people in their neighborhood."

Lorka Muñoz has found that all kinds of people join Dayton's community gardens—young children, teenagers, parents, and grandparents. They all have one thing in common. They want to make their neighborhoods better places to live.

Getting a gardening group together and finding an empty lot are the first steps in creating a community garden. Then the fun begins. "The people at GWYN and the gardeners design the garden," says Muñoz.

Each garden has two parts. One is a community space—an area that everyone can use. Muñoz helps the gardeners choose trees and ground covers to plant there. The rest of the garden is divided into small plots where each gardener can plant flowers and vegetables.

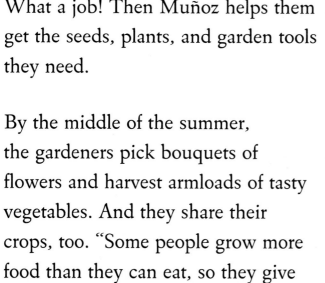

Before the planting can begin, the gardeners work together to clean up the lot. They haul away trash, dig up rocks, pull weeds, and prepare the soil. What a job! Then Muñoz helps them get the seeds, plants, and garden tools they need.

By the middle of the summer, the gardeners pick bouquets of flowers and harvest armloads of tasty vegetables. And they share their crops, too. "Some people grow more food than they can eat, so they give away the extra," says Muñoz.

Lorka Muñoz believes that community gardens help neighborhoods in many ways. "People grow their own fresh food," she says. "Neighbors meet each other and begin to work together. And best of all, the neighborhood looks better."

Lorka Muñoz's
Tips for Improving Your Community

1 Decide exactly what you want to improve.

2 Share your idea with other interested people.

3 Ask for help. Parents or other adults may be willing to lend a hand.

4 Get started. Make a plan, and then carry it out.

How to
Make a Public-Service Poster

community
group's project

Communities are always trying to improve themselves. Some have cleanup days. Others plant community gardens. How do communities advertise projects or events like these? One way is to make public-service posters.

What is a public-service poster? A public-service poster is a large printed sign. It has information about a public concern or event. It may be colorfully illustrated.

Interested in joining…

Linden Heights Neighborhood Garden?

Find out how…

Come to a garden
planning meeting
Thursday, July 6
St. Anthony School Cafeteria
6:30 - 7:00 p.m.

Sponsored by:
Grow With Your Neighbors
of Wegerzyn Horticultural Center
S.E. Priority Board
Linden Heights Community Council
City of Dayton, Dept. of Planning

the event that is
being advertised

place

time

organization
that made the
poster

colorful
decorations

1 Choose an Event

Form a group with several classmates. Decide on an event that will help your community. The event can be a real one that happens in your school or town. It can also be an event that you would like to see happen.

Here are different community events.

TOOLS

- paper and pencil
- posterboard
- marking pens, paints, or colored pencils

- festivals
- cleanup campaigns
- bake sales
- canned-food drives

2 Design the Poster

Your group has chosen an event to announce. Now you can design your poster.

- Decide what you want the poster to say.
- Figure out how it will look. What pictures do you want to go with the words?
- What colors do you want to use?

On a sheet of paper, make a sketch of your design. Do you have all the information you need? Do you like the way it looks?

3 Make a Poster

Now you can make your public-service poster. Decide who will write the words and who will draw the pictures. Remember, neatness counts! When you have finished, take a close look. Are all the words spelled correctly? Have you included the time and place?

Tip A public-service poster may tell community members what they need to bring to an event.

4 Show and Tell

Display your poster in your classroom. Answer any questions your classmates have. Look at their posters, too. How many different kinds of events are advertised? Which events do you think are important?

If You Are Using a Computer ...

Create your poster on the computer, using borders and clip art. Remember to experiment with font size and style to make your poster look great.

THINK

People do all kinds of things to help their communities. What kinds of things would you like to do?

Lorka Muñoz
Community Garden Director ▶

A community grows through the contributions of newcomers.

New Horizons

Discover some of the contributions that immigrants have made to our country.

Learn how Mary McLeod Bethune enriched a community in Florida. Find out how some kids honored her for what she did.

WORKSHOP 2

Contribute one of your favorite recipes to a community cookbook.

Family Biscuits

2 cups all-purpose flour
1 tablespoon baking powder
1 teaspoon salt
1/3 cup shortening
3/4 cup milk

1. Heat oven to 425°F.

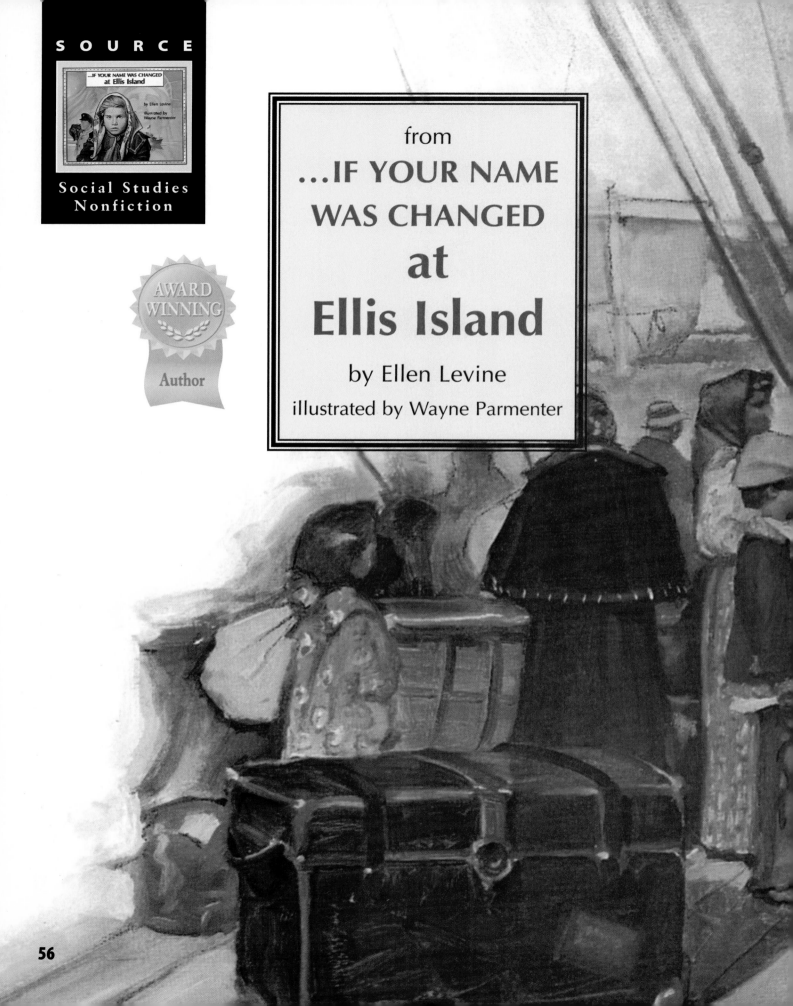

from
...IF YOUR NAME
WAS CHANGED
at
Ellis Island

by Ellen Levine

illustrated by Wayne Parmenter

From 1892 to 1924, over twelve million immigrants came to the United States from Europe. For most of these newcomers, Ellis Island was the first stop in America. This immigration center was located in New York harbor. Doctors and legal inspectors checked all the immigrants. A few unlucky ones were sent home. But most entered the United States, and many became American citizens.

Why did people come to America?

Many people believed that America was a "Golden Land"—a place where you could get a decent job, go to a free school, and eat well. There was a saying in Polish that people came to America *za chlebem*—"for bread." One person added that they came "for bread, with butter."

In Russia, six-year-old Alec Bodanis was told that in America, "you'll become a millionaire in no time. Take a shovel with you because they shovel gold from the streets." No one knows how these stories began, but Margot Matyshek, age eleven when she left Germany, had also heard that in America, "the streets are paved with gold. And if you wish for candy, it drops from the sky right into your mouth!"

Some people came to look for work. Wages were higher in America than in their home countries. Until the late 1800s, businesses often sent agents overseas to encourage workers to migrate. If you agreed to work for their companies, they would pay your way to America.

Many people came because land was cheap and plentiful. In 1862, the U.S. government passed a law

called the Homestead Act. Newcomers could stake a claim to 160 acres of land. After five years of living on and working the land, they'd pay a small amount of money, and the acres would be theirs. Railroad companies also owned a great deal of land in the west. They sent agents to foreign countries offering this land for sale at good prices.

Some governments of the new western states advertised in European newspapers about their growing towns and cheap farmland. They wanted new settlers. Often the advertisements were not true. They showed pictures of towns that didn't exist, and gave descriptions of farm fields where forests stood. But people came anyway. Searching, always searching, for a better life.

A Swedish song had these words about America:

> "Ducks and chickens rain right down,
> A roasted goose flies in,
> And on the table lands one more
> with knife and fork stuck in."

Who could find a better place?

What did people bring with them?

Usually whatever they could carry. Some had
suitcases and trunks. Most had bundles tied together
with string. People carried baskets, cardboard boxes,
tins, leather sacks—any type of container you could
imagine.

They often brought their feather quilts,
mattresses, and pillows, for the steamships just
provided thin blankets. They packed fancy clothes,
specially embroidered and crocheted. Sometimes
people wore layers of all their clothing so they
wouldn't have to pack them. Often they brought food
for the long trip over the ocean, like smoked sausages
or hams, or other foods they thought they couldn't
get in America.

Many people had to sell or give away almost
everything they owned in order to travel to the new
land. But sometimes they were able to bring their
favorite things. One young girl mailed her dolls to her
relatives in America before she herself came. Another
brought a book of fairy tales, which she carried in a
basket she held tightly for the whole trip.

How long would the ocean trip take?

Until the mid-1800s, most people came to America on sailing ships. These usually took about forty days to cross the Atlantic Ocean, but sometimes it could take up to six months. By the late 1800s, steamships had replaced sailing ships, and the trip was much faster. If there were no bad storms or other problems, the trip usually took anywhere from six to thirty-two days.

Where would you go when you landed at Ellis Island?

When the barge pulled up to the dock at Ellis Island, immigrants walked under the entry arches into the ground-floor baggage room where some left their luggage. Others held on to all their bags. One baggage worker said he could recognize what country people had come from by the type of luggage they carried and by the way they tied the knots around their bundles.

Then they went up a staircase into the Registry Room, also known as the Great Hall. There they would be examined again by doctors and then by immigration inspectors.

As they reached the top of the stairs, the Great Hall spread out before them like a huge maze. Metal pipes divided the space into narrow aisles, and sections were enclosed in wire mesh. One young immigrant said, "You think you're in a zoo!" After 1911, the iron pipes were removed and replaced by long rows of wooden benches.

Hundreds, at times thousands, of immigrants passed through the Great Hall. The noise, some said, was like the Tower of Babel—sometimes thirty languages being spoken at the same time.

Ellis Island was like a miniature city for immigrants. There were waiting rooms, dormitories for over a thousand people, restaurants, a hospital, baggage room, post office, banks to change foreign money, a railroad ticket office, medical and legal examination rooms, baths, laundries, office areas for charities and church groups, and courtrooms.

Ellis Island was the last hurdle you had to pass before you were to enter the country.

What contributions have immigrants made?

From the time of America's founding, new immigrants have played an important role. Eight of the fifty-five men who signed the Declaration of Independence were born in other countries. And when Thomas Jefferson wrote in the Declaration that "all men are created equal," he used the words of his Italian-born friend Philip Mazzei.

History books often list famous Americans who were immigrants. These lists usually include Albert Einstein, the German-Jewish scientist; Alexander Graham Bell, from Scotland, who invented the telephone; Elizabeth Blackwell, English-born, the first woman doctor in America; Knute Rockne, the Norwegian football player and coach; Marcus Garvey, from Jamaica, the leader of the Back-to-Africa movement; Greta Garbo, the Swedish movie star; Spyros Skouras, the Greek movie producer; Irving Berlin, the Russian-Jewish composer and songwriter; Enrico Fermi, the Italian scientist, and many others.

But millions of immigrants, not just the "famous" ones, created or started things that we think of as totally American. We take these things for granted, but they are the contributions of immigrants:

—log cabins first built by Swedes;

—symphony orchestras and glee clubs organized by Germans;

—movies produced in
America by Russian Jews
and Greeks;

—Santa Claus, bowling, and
ice-skating from the Dutch.

Many peoples contributed to American English.
"Yankee" is a Dutch word, and "alligator" is Spanish.
"Phooey" is from German, and "prairie" is French.
"Jukebox" is African, and "gung ho" is Chinese. And
there are hundreds more words that were originally
foreign and are now part of the English language.

If you think of Native American Indians as the first
immigrants, then the names of many states come from
Indian "immigrant" languages: Arizona, Wisconsin,
Wyoming, Connecticut, Mississippi, and Oklahoma, to
name a few. "Raccoon," "skunk," and "succotash" also
are Indian words.

As Abraham Lincoln said, immigrants have been
"a source of national wealth and strength."

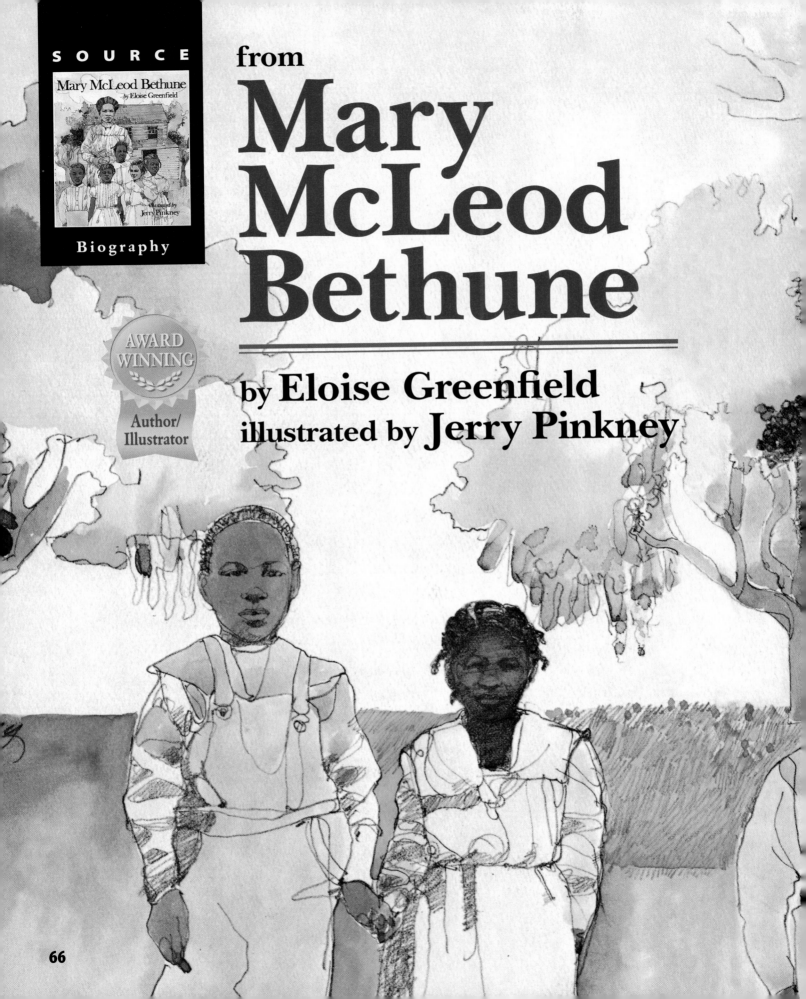

from

Mary McLeod Bethune

by **Eloise Greenfield**
illustrated by **Jerry Pinkney**

As a child, Mary McLeod Bethune dreamed of going to school and learning to read. She finally got her chance in 1886, when she was 11 years old. Emma Wilson and Lucy Laney, both teachers, helped Mary make her dream come true. Once Mary Bethune was on her way, she kept right on going until she became a teacher, too.

A few years after she began teaching, Mary met Albertus Bethune, also a teacher, who became her husband. The following year, their son, Albert, was born.

When Albert was five years old, Mary Bethune made a big decision. She wanted to start a school of her own. She thought of Miss Laney and Miss Wilson, and she remembered herself as a child longing to learn. There were many black children like her who lived in places without schools. They had questions but no answers. They wanted to learn and she wanted to teach them.

She heard about Daytona Beach, Florida, where a new railroad was being built. The workmen who were putting down the railroad track were not being paid enough. They lived with their families in camps that were too crowded. There were no schools. Mrs. Bethune decided that she would go there.

When Mrs. Bethune arrived in Daytona Beach, she had only one dollar and fifty cents. She stayed with a friend, and every day she went for a walk, looking for a building that she could use as a school. Finally, she found an old two-story cottage. The owner said he would rent it to her for eleven dollars a month. He agreed to wait a few weeks until she could raise the first month's rent.

Mrs. Bethune visited the homes of black families, telling them about her school. Neighbors came to paint the cottage and to fix the broken steps. Children helped with the cleaning.

On an autumn day in 1904, Mrs. Bethune stood in the doorway of the cottage, smiling and ringing a bell. It was time for school to start. Five little girls came in and took their seats. The school was named the Daytona Normal and Industrial School for Girls. It was an elementary school, and Albert would learn there, too, until he was older.

Mrs. Bethune and the students used wooden boxes as desks and chairs. They burned logs and used the charcoal as pencils. They mashed berries and used the juice as ink.

The children loved the school. Some of them lived there with Mrs. Bethune. All of them wanted to help raise money for the rent and for the books and paper and lamps and beds that they needed.

After classes, they made ice cream and pies to sell. The children peeled and mashed sweet potatoes while Mrs. Bethune rolled the crust. They gave programs at hotels and in churches. The children sang and recited. Mrs. Bethune spoke to the audiences about the school. She bought a secondhand bicycle and rode all over Daytona Beach, knocking on doors and asking people for their help.

Many people gave. Some of them were rich, and some of them did not have much money themselves but were willing to share the little that they had.

When too many children wanted to attend and a larger building was needed, adults in the community again gave their time and work. They took away the trash from the land that Mrs. Bethune bought. Those who were carpenters helped to put the building up. Those who were gardeners planted flowers and trees around it.

Mrs. Bethune named the new building Faith Hall in honor of her favorite building at Scotia Seminary. She had faith in God, in herself, and in black people. Over the door she hung a sign that said "Enter to learn."

Across from Faith Hall, Mrs. Bethune started a small farm. The students planted fruits and vegetables to use and to sell. They grew strawberries, tomatoes, string beans, carrots, and corn. They grew sugar cane to make syrup.

As the years passed, more students came to the school, and more teachers. More buildings were added. Albert went away to school, but Mrs. Bethune was busier than ever. Almost every day a new problem arose that she had to solve.

One day, a student became very ill. Because there was no hospital for blacks for many, many miles, Mrs. Bethune rushed her to the nearest white hospital. The doctors agreed to take care of her, but not inside the hospital. They put the patient on the back porch with a screen around her bed.

Mrs. Bethune was very angry, but there was nothing she could do. The student was too sick to be moved to another hospital. But when the girl was well, Mrs. Bethune decided that someone had to start a hospital for blacks in Daytona Beach, and she would do it. She started a little two-bed hospital which later had twenty beds. She named it McLeod Hospital in memory of her father, who had died. It saved many black lives.

Later that same year, one of Mrs. Bethune's brothers came for his first visit. He walked around the campus with his sister and visited classrooms where young people were being taught to use their minds and their hands. The choir sang for him. He was proud of his sister and of all that he saw and heard, and Mrs. Bethune was proud to show him what had been done.

Kids Honor

Mary McLeod Bethune

A class in New York City was talking about streets in their neighborhood named after famous African Americans. They discovered several streets that were named after African-American men, such as Martin Luther King, Jr. and Malcolm X.

But there were no streets named after African-American women. The class decided to do something about it.

The students did research about great African-American women and studied maps of the city. Then they voted for a woman and a street. They chose Mary McLeod Bethune because she spent her whole life bringing education to African Americans. In fact, their school is named after her. The class decided to change the name of 134th Street, which runs in front of the building. That way, the students could see the results of their hard work every day. "They can feel a sense of ownership in their community," their teacher said.

The students had to ask their community board and New York's City Council to change the street's name. At a meeting with the City Council, one boy from the class made their case. He said, "We are here today to follow in Mary McLeod Bethune's footsteps. When we learned that there wasn't one street in Harlem named after an African-American woman, we didn't just get mad. We did something about it!"

About a year later, the members of the City Council voted to rename the street. Now New York City has a Mary McLeod Bethune Place, and a class has a lot to be proud of.

A class gathers around a sculpture of Mary McLeod Bethune. Thanks to these students, a street has been named after her.

How to

Make a Community Recipe Book

How do people in communities learn about each other? One way is by sharing favorite foods. Some communities even put together community recipe books. The recipe books may contain old recipes, recipes from other countries, or family favorites.

What is a recipe book? A recipe book contains a collection of recipes for foods. A recipe is a list of ingredients and directions for making a food or drink.

title of recipe tells the kind of food you are making

ingredients you need to make the food

directions for putting the ingredients together

a paragraph that tells why this food is important to you

YOU MIGHT MAKE A FRIEND ALONG THE WAY

When I was about 7 or 8 years old, I'd come home from school and find my grandmother baking those delicious oversized biscuits. A platter of them would be on top of the stove to keep warm. I'd sneak up to the stove and grab a biscuit then run outside to play. She always caught me, pulled me back by my shirttail and said, "Where are you going?" I'd tell her I was going outside to play. Then she would hand me another biscuit and say, "You'd better take two because you might make a friend along the way."

Phil Mendez
Los Angeles, CA

Family Biscuits

2 cups all-purpose flour
1 tablespoon baking powder
1 teaspoon salt
1/3 cup shortening
3/4 cup milk

1. Heat oven to 425°F.

2. Combine flour, baking powder and salt in large bowl. Mix in shortening until it forms coarse crumbs. Add milk. Mix with fork. Form dough into ball.

3. Put dough on lightly floured surface. Knead gently 8 to 10 times. Roll dough to 1/2-inch thickness. Cut with floured 2-inch round cutter. Place on ungreased baking sheet.

4. Bake at 425°F for 12 to 14 minutes.

Makes 12 to 16 biscuits.

1 Choose a Recipe

Think of a special food that you like—one that you want to share with your classmates. It might be a recipe that has been in your family for years. You might eat it only on holidays or special occasions. Or it might be a food that your family likes and prepares often. Bring the recipe to class.

Here are some different kinds of foods to choose recipes for:

- salads

- breads

- vegetables

- meat or fish dishes

- pasta

- desserts

2 Talk Food

Now you have a recipe. Write a few sentences telling why it is important to you. You may have a happy memory about this food. If it's a holiday food, there may be a story that goes with it. The food may remind you of a special person you know.

3 Write the Recipe

Now you are ready to copy your recipe and your story about it onto a clean sheet of paper. Write down the ingredients and directions carefully. Make sure you have copied everything correctly so that the recipe will come out right. Include your story and write your name at the bottom.

You may wish to decorate your recipe.

Tip Some recipes need special cooking tools. Be sure you include these tools in your recipe's directions.

4 It's a Book!

Put all the recipes together to make your community recipe book. Work with your classmates to design a cover. You may want to group similar recipes together. When you have finished, talk about the recipes in your book. Which ones do you know? Which ones are new? Which ones would you like to try?

If You Are Using a Computer ...

Draft your recipe on the computer and decorate it with a special border. You also can create a table of contents for your cookbook on the computer.

THINK

Everyone in a community has different ideas. Why do you think sharing recipes and food is a good way to bring members of a community together?

Lorca Muñoz
Community Garden Director ▶

A community is strengthened by preserving landmarks and traditions.

Keepsakes

Watch two friends spring into action to save a special tree. Learn how a group of kids in Massachusetts became heroes of the environment.

Grab your partner and dance to the music of a South American *carnaval*. Chill out at a winter celebration, too.

PROJECT

Design one of the squares in a community quilt.

SQUIRREL PARK

BY
LISA CAMPBELL ERNST

To most people in Springdale, Chuck and Stuart were an unlikely pair of best friends.

Sure, they had their differences. But they also had a lot in common. Like climbing trees, collecting leaves, and—most importantly—loving the ancient, gnarled oak tree that grew in the center of town.

For Chuck the magnificent tree was *home*. He grew up in its strong branches, and he played, ate, and slept there.

As the town of Springdale grew, its old trees were chopped down one by one, to make room for new buildings. Finally, Chuck's was the last giant to escape the builder's plans.

Even as the other squirrels left town for more trees, Chuck remained loyal. "This tree is my home," he insisted. "Forever."

Stuart loved the tree as well, from the smell of its fresh new buds in spring, to the veiny old bark that told of the tree's long history.

It was Stuart's father—Mr. Ivey—who had built the new buildings in town, and they were just like him: big, straight, and powerful. Stuart was none of those things.

"Out with the old, in with the new!" Mr. Ivey thundered as the trees were cut down to make room for his buildings. "Someday, Stuart, you will follow in my footsteps!" Mr. Ivey told his son.

Stuart shuddered at the thought. "I promise I'll protect your tree," he told Chuck, "no matter what."

Then one morning Stuart's father broke the calm. "STUART!" he roared from the base of the tree.

"Yes, Dad?" Stuart called timidly.

Mr. Ivey frowned. "Son, you know I don't approve of you lollygagging here with that—that *rodent*," he shouted, "but since you insist, I've decided . . . we will build a park here."

Mr. Ivey rushed on. "This is your first job, Stuart. *You* will design the park."

"But how?" Stuart asked.

"Draw a picture," Mr. Ivey instructed, "of how the park should look. You will show your drawing at the town meeting this Saturday. Then the park will be built just that way."

Mr. Ivey turned to leave. "This is an important job, son," he called back. "Don't let me down."

At first Chuck and Stuart just stared at each other in disbelief. "A park!" Stuart shouted at last, and the two friends began to dance around the tree. Chuck leapt and twirled.

"We'll plant a hundred *more* trees!" cried Stuart. "Walnut! Pecan! Chestnut! And we'll make nature paths, and a playground . . ."

Chuck looked up into the mass of swaying, dancing leaves above him. And just for a second, he could have sworn he saw the tree smile.

The next morning, Chuck and Stuart got busy—Saturday's town meeting was two days away. Drawing their plot of land, Stuart filled pages with curving, curling paths, with playgrounds and flowers. Chuck dipped his paws in green ink and marked where each tree would be planted. At the center of it all, they drew their spectacular tree.

"Perfect," Stuart said proudly. And Chuck agreed.

Suddenly, though, Mr. Ivey burst into the room. "I see I'm just in time!" he roared, and thrust a strange-looking box into Stuart's hands.

"For your drawing!" Mr. Ivey shouted, taking out two strange wooden tools and sweeping Chuck and Stuart's artwork off the table.

Mr. Ivey demonstrated how to slide a pencil along the edge of one tool to draw a flat, straight line. With the other tool, he drew straight lines at an angle, and straight lines up and down.

"Beautiful!" Mr. Ivey sang. "*You* will demonstrate these tools at the town meeting. Like father, like son!"

"But—" Stuart began, "I thought curved paths would look nice with the tree." Chuck quickly nodded.

"Nonsense!" Mr. Ivey barked on his way out the door. "With all of my straight buildings in town, I need a park to match."

Stuart stared blankly at Mr. Ivey's drawing and tools. "Now what?" he asked glumly.

Chuck led him back to the tree, in answer.

Unrolling the drawing there, Stuart discovered Mr. Ivey had drawn paths straight through the tree. "We'll have to change that," Stuart gasped, curving the paths around it.

As Chuck chattered his approval, Stuart drew more: playgrounds and curving paths mixed in with Mr. Ivey's straight ones. Soon Chuck got busy with the green ink. And again, at the center of it all, they drew their fabulous tree.

The next morning, Chuck and Stuart bounded into Mr. Ivey's office with their drawing.

"Our park!" Stuart proudly sang. "For tomorrow's town meeting!"

Mr. Ivey frowned at what he saw.

"We used some of the straight lines from your tools," Stuart quickly pointed out, explaining about the path through the tree, "and added our own curved ones—"

"But the tools' lines were *perfect*!" Mr. Ivey interrupted. "Who cares about that old tree?"

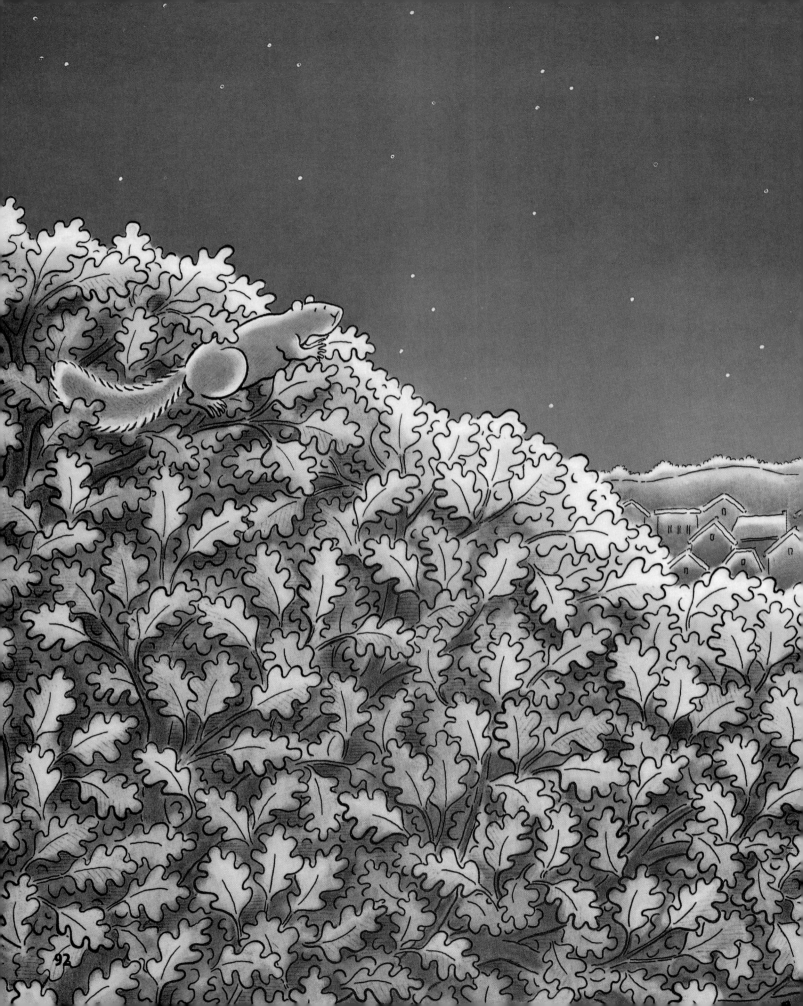

Hearing that, Chuck leapt to his feet. CRASH! Three bottles of ink toppled over.

"Out!" Mr. Ivey shouted as the ink swam across their artwork. "Both of you! I'll do a new drawing myself!"

Stuart's father sent him straight home, so Chuck sat alone, at the top of the tree.

"Don't worry," was the last thing Stuart had said.

But Chuck *was* worried. He could still hear Mr. Ivey's voice asking, "Who cares about that old tree?"

"*I* do!" Chuck now called out. "*I* care!" By nightfall, Chuck was frantic.

Suddenly, Chuck saw Mr. Ivey leave his office, carrying the tools and his new drawing. Disappearing into the town hall, he reappeared moments later, empty-handed.

Chuck now sprang into action.

Racing to the town hall, Chuck squeezed through the mail slot. "That drawing is here somewhere," he said.

And he was right. There in the great hall, it sat with Mr. Ivey's tools and art supplies, ready for the demonstration. Chuck inched past the rows of empty chairs until one giant leap landed him square in the middle of the park drawing.

He quickly surveyed the park at his feet—straight paths, a puny playground, no flowers at all. But it was not until Chuck moved off the center of the drawing that he realized the worst: *His tree was not there.*

Chuck could not believe his eyes. He frantically searched the paper—surely the tree was somewhere. But it was not. His tree was to be cut down.

"Don't panic," Chuck told himself. "*Do* something."

First Chuck rolled up Mr. Ivey's drawing and buried it in the pot of a fern nearby. "That takes care of that," he announced.

But turning around, Chuck eyed the tools and art supplies. "He'll make another one," Chuck realized, "just like it."

"Unless . . ." Chuck said, picking up a wooden tool and smelling it. "Maybe . . ." Suddenly the town hall was filled with a sound that would continue all through the night.

The sound of nibbling.

When Stuart and his father arrived at the town hall the next morning, an excited crowd waited.

Mr. Ivey strode proudly to the front. "Ladies and gentlemen!" he called. "I present . . . your park!" And with that, he turned to reach for his drawing.

Suddenly, the fast-talking Mr. Ivey was speechless. "The—the *tools*," he stammered at last. "My *drawing*!" A paper with Chuck's tree—drawn on with tiny green pawprints—lay there. Mr. Ivey turned white.

As the hushed crowd waited expectantly, Stuart spied Chuck hiding in the potted fern, and understood. "May I have your attention," Stuart timidly called, rushing forward.

All eyes now turned to Stuart.
"My father," he quietly began,
"has made many wonderful
buildings in Springdale—and
now a park. Today he has asked
me to demonstrate his new tools,
created specially for this important
park design."

The townspeople clapped,
and Mr. Ivey, still dumbstruck,
stood silently by. Sliding his pencil
along one tool, Stuart began to
draw curving, curling paths around
Chuck's tree.

As the drawing grew, Stuart
talked—about flowers, playgrounds,
and nature paths, of new trees and
the hope for more squirrels. Mostly,
though, he talked about the amazing,
ancient tree that was older than the
town itself.

By the time Stuart was finished,
the townspeople—and Chuck—had
jumped to their feet, cheering.

But all of this time, Mr. Ivey
stood by, silently watching,
listening.

"Mr. Ivey!" the mayor finally
called. "Speak to us of your very
unusual, very beautiful design!"

Slowly Mr. Ivey stepped forward, first looking at the smiling townspeople, then at the drawing. He shook his head, he hunched his shoulders, he waved his arms. At last he turned to Stuart. "What can I say?" he whispered. "Only my very unusual son could make such an unusual drawing. But you are right. It *is* beautiful."

The townspeople—and Chuck—cheered again.

The park was, indeed, built just like Chuck and Stuart's design. In fact, it became so loved, that soon towns all across the country wanted parks the same. Stuart and Mr. Ivey were quick to oblige, using Chuck's very special tools.

With the passing years, Stuart and Chuck could still be found sitting happily in their grand old tree. From its branches they watched as the other trees grew, and squirrels arrived to make their homes. At last the park, with its squirrels, became so treasured that the townspeople affectionately named it Squirrel Park.

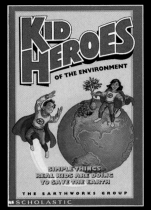

S O U R C E

Environmental
Handbook

from **KID HEROES OF THE ENVIRONMENT**

PROTECTING

by
**The
EarthWorks
Group**

A PARK

KID HEROES

Names: Kate Crowther, Sarah Crowther, Laura Sheppard-Brick, Ariana Wohl

Ages: 9–10

Grade: 5

Town: Northampton, Massachusetts

School: Jackson Street School

Goal: Protect trees in a local park

WHAT THEY DID

Summary

In 1989, the Northampton department of public works decided to cut down 12 full-grown trees in Childs Park to make a road wider and add parking spaces.

When Sarah and Kate heard the news, they told their friends Ariana and Laura about it.

All of them were concerned. Ariana pointed out that trees help keep our air clean. Sarah was concerned because animals like squirrels and birds would lose their homes. She says, "It was hard to imagine that one day there would be a park, and the next day there would be parking spaces."

The girls agreed: They had to stop the project; they would do whatever it took. Within days, they were staging a protest in front of the park.

Results

The park was saved, and the street was left as it was. And, Laura says, "I think a lot of the kids in this town have become more environmentally conscious as a result."

HOW THEY DID IT

1. They considered their options. Sarah's mother suggested they picket—hold up signs at the park—and they liked the idea. They also decided to write letters to the mayor and start a petition.

2. They made signs saying, "Save our trees, save our animals!" and "If you care, please honk your horn!"

3. They asked their friends to help picket, but they didn't let adults participate. "We wanted it to be strictly a kids' event," says Ariana. They called their group Community Children to Save Our Park (CCSOP).

4. They picketed for 2 days. Sarah says, "People were

very supportive: we got about 500 honks."

5. As a result of the picketing, the mayor came to Laura's house and met with the neighbors and protesters. Some people—like the engineer who did the plans for the wider street—opposed saving the park. He said, "An intersection is forever, a tree can always be planted again." But in the end, most people agreed with the kids.

YOU CAN BE A HERO

• "Don't be afraid to tell people what you think," says Laura. "One kid's father told us to wait until fall to picket. We said they were going to cut down the trees in two weeks, so we didn't want to take any chances."

• "Don't be afraid to tell the media what you're doing," says Laura. "I was scared to tell our local newspaper about our plans,

because the article I'd read made it sound like the trees were already doomed. But the newspaper people aren't in charge. They just want news."

• How do you deal with the people who are against what you're doing? Laura says, "If they don't have much power, just ignore them. If they do, try to get someone more powerful on your side. In our case it was the mayor."

TONIGHT

Illustrated with *arpilleras* sewn by the Club de Madres Virgen del Carmen of Lima, Peru

IS CARNAVAL

BY ARTHUR DORROS

"Wake up, sleepyhead," my mother is calling. But I'm already awake. I'm thinking about Carnaval. This year I will play the *quena*, a flute, with my father in the band. "The quena is the voice of the band—the singer of the band," says Papa. Papa plays with the band every year at Carnaval. People in costumes will parade and dance to the music for three whole days and nights.

Carnaval is in the big village down the valley, and it's only three days away!

"We have a lot of work to do before then," Papa says. We work all year, almost every day, but not during Carnaval!

We get up each day before it is light outside, there is so much to do. Mama takes my little sister, Teresa, to the river to get water. Today Mama washes clothes, too. Papa and I look for firewood to use for cooking. Sometimes we walk a long way to find wood—there are hardly any trees in the high Andes Mountains of South America, where we live.

Today I bring my quena along, so I can practice special songs for Carnaval. A lot of the songs have a good beat that makes you want to dance. *Tunk tunk, tunk tunk.* Papa's ax chopping a log sounds like the beat of the *bombo*, the drum he will play with the band.

Back home Teresa drops kernels of corn into an empty pot. Mama will boil the corn for our meal. *Pling pling, pling pling pling.* The kernels make sounds like the strings of Uncle Pablo's *charango*. He will play in the band with us too, at Carnaval.

After our meal, we get a field ready for planting. I lead the oxen, to make sure they plow straight. Mama follows us and picks stones out of the loose earth. After Carnaval, my friend Paco and his family will help us plant potatoes. Sometimes Paco's family helps us in our field, and other times we help them in theirs. One of the songs I'm practicing for Carnaval is about working in the fields with friends.

After we plow, I take the hungry llamas high into the mountains to find grass. The best grass is by the crumbling walls of buildings made hundreds of years ago when the Incas ruled these mountains. No one knows how the giant stones were cut to fit together so well. Sometimes we use the old stones to build walls and houses and even terraces for the fields.

I sit on a wall and play my quena. I play a song called *"Mis Llamitas,"* "My Little Llamas," and the llamas leap and dance around. I imagine they are dancing to my music.

The wind whistling across the stones sounds like the windy notes of a *zampoña*, a panpipe. I will play my quena and Paco will play his zampoña when we meet at Carnaval. That's one of the things I like about Carnaval—we get together with friends from our mountain and from all around the valley.

One day is gone. Now we have only today and tomorrow before tomorrow night—when Carnaval begins. I can hardly wait. This morning Papa shears wool from an alpaca. An alpaca is like a llama, but with softer wool. I carry the wool to Mama, so she can spin it into yarn. "You don't have to run," laughs Mama. "Carnaval will come as soon as it can."

Mama's fingers twirl the wool round and round. She can spin yarn while she's walking, or selling vegetables, or doing almost anything. When she has enough yarn, she'll color it with different dyes. Grandma will weave it into cloth of many colors. Then Mama will cut and sew the cloth to make us clothes. Maybe she'll make me a new jacket.

In the afternoon, we dig potatoes out of the damp earth in a field we planted months ago. The digging usually makes me tired, but today I keep working as fast as I can to help harvest all the potatoes. Tomorrow we'll take them down into the valley to sell at the market. And after the market is cleared away, Carnaval will begin!

We gather red potatoes; yellow, black, and brown potatoes; even purple potatoes. In the Andes, we have hundreds of different kinds of potatoes.

We drop our potatoes into burlap bags, *plonk, plonk, plonk*. The llamas help carry the heavy bags to Antonio's truck. Antonio came from the village today, and he will sleep tonight in his truck.

Finally. Today we take the potatoes to market—then tonight is Carnaval!

I wait and wait to hear the truck start. The motor coughs and groans, *errr errr errr*. But at last Antonio gets it started. Mama, Papa, Teresa, and I—and the potatoes—bounce along in the back of the old truck, which rattles and shakes down the mountain. It stops like a bus to pick up people carrying onions, beans, carrots, turnips, peas, and peppers; llama wool; clothes; and food they have made for Carnaval.

"Hey," I hear someone say, "don't let that chicken eat our corn. We're taking it to market."

The truck bounces over a big bump. I reach down to make sure my quena is not broken. I want people to hear my quena sing when I play at Carnaval.

"Watch out flying over those bumps, Antonio," someone shouts. "Will this old truck fly us to the village?"

"Don't worry," Antonio shouts back. "This old truck and I know how to get there."

People hug when they climb into the truck. We don't see these friends very often. We all stand and look out along the way. People throw water balloons and water from buckets to try to splash us. They're excited about Carnaval.

At the market, I help unload the heavy bags of potatoes, and then I walk around. I love to see the brightly colored piles of vegetables. People trade wool that still smells like llamas or sheep. And the nutty smell of toasted fava beans and corn makes my mouth water.

But today I can't wait until Mama sells all of our potatoes and the market is cleared away. Then people will come out in their costumes. At first it will be hard to see who each person is—many of the people will be wearing masks. I'll find the band. Papa's bombo will start booming, Paco's zampoña will be whistling, and Uncle Pablo's charango plinging. People will start shouting "Play your songs," stamping their feet, swirling, turning, dancing to the music faster and faster because—

TONIGHT IS CARNAVAL.

When I play my quena with the band, people start to sing. My quena sings and the people sing. I play the special songs I've learned for Carnaval, about llamas, mountains, and friends. We play songs with a beat for dancing. Paco and I watch all the people hold onto each other in one long line that dances—laughing, winding through the village.

Our band plays under the moon and flickering stars, and we will play until the sun comes up. We play the songs of our mountain days and nights . . . for tonight is Carnaval.

HOW ARPILLERAS ARE MADE

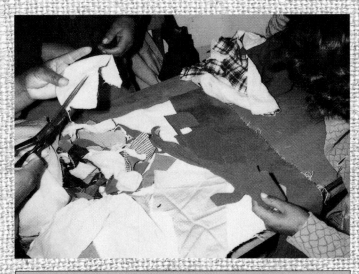

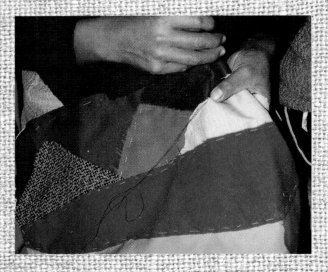

An arpillera-maker draws the design on white cloth. Pieces of cloth are selected and cut to fit the design.

Big pieces of cloth are sewn on to form the background.

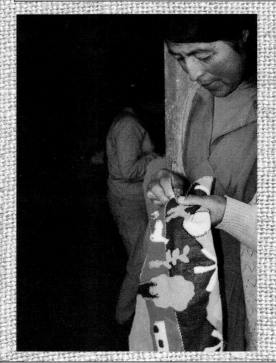

The edges of each shape are neatly stitched, and details are added by sewing on more pieces of cut cloth and by embroidering.

Dolls and other three-dimensional objects (vegetables, musical instruments) are made . . .

Another arpillera is finished.

. . . and sewn onto the arpillera.

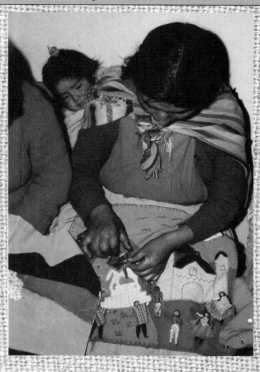

Arpillera-makers often work together in groups. These members of the Club de Madres Virgen del Carmen are making vegetables and dolls for arpilleras. With money from the sale of arpilleras, the group also runs a kitchen that helps feed two to three hundred people a day.

CARNIVAL

In 1885, a newspaper reporter was visiting Saint Paul, Minnesota. He took one look at all the snow, felt the icy wind blowing, and wrote, "No right-minded person would ever come here in the winter!" The people of Saint Paul decided to prove that reporter wrong. Every winter, MILLIONS of visitors flock to the snowy city. What's the attraction? Saint Paul's Winter Carnival, of course! It's the nation's oldest winter carnival, first held in 1886. And it's so much fun that no one even notices the cold!

The giant ice palace is always a favorite with Winter Carnival visitors. It took several weeks and 30,000 huge blocks of ice to build this sparkling castle.

IN THE SNOW

▲ Even a reindeer visited Saint Paul's first
Winter Carnival in 1886.

▲ Each year, a new Winter Carnival button is the ticket to all the fun. ▼

The Legend of the Winter Carnival

A long, long time ago, Boreas, King of all the Winds, discovered Saint Paul—a beautiful ice-covered city in Minnesota. "This frozen wonderland will be my winter capital!" he declared. To celebrate, King Boreas and his queen held a winter carnival in their new home. There were twelve days of feasting and fun for everyone.

But not everyone was happy about the celebration. Boreas's enemy, Vulcanus, King of Fire, hated ice and snow. "Away with winter!" he bellowed. "It's time for spring!"

Vulcanus and his followers plotted to drive King Boreas out of Saint Paul. On the last day of the carnival, Vulcanus stormed into the Boreas's ice castle. To keep the peace, King Boreas agreed to leave. And so the warmth of springtime returned to Saint Paul. However, each year Boreas returns, and he brings another winter carnival with him!

▲ Speedskating is just one of the fun winter sports that take place during the Winter Carnival.

▲ Artists use chainsaws and chisels to create fantastic ice carvings. Over a million people brave the cold weather each year to see the frozen sculptures.

▲ From late January to early February, glistening ice sculptures turn downtown Saint Paul into a winter wonderland.

How to Create a Community Quilt

Design a quilt *that tells* all about *your community.*

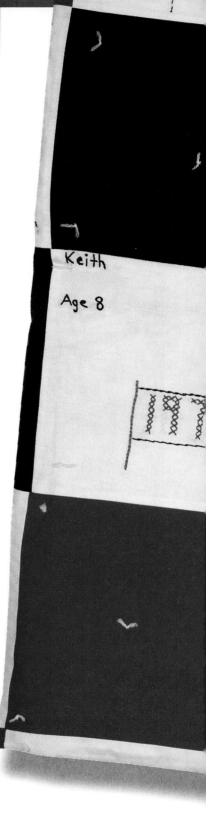

Have you ever seen a community quilt? It's a special patchwork wall hanging that celebrates the good things about a community. On a community quilt you may see pictures of famous landmarks, community events, beautiful parks, or important people. You may even find words written on it. Many of these special quilts are beautiful works of art. But they also show why communities are great places to live.

1 Choose a Subject

With your classmates, list the things that make your community unlike any other. These may include people, places, events, or activities. Choose the part of your community that you want to show on a quilt square.

Special parts of your community might be:

- famous landmarks such as statues or buildings
- city, state, or national parks
- community groups
- places that people use, such as libraries or playfields
- celebrations and parades
- people, such as the mayor

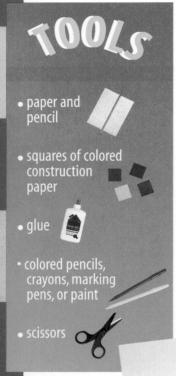

TOOLS

- paper and pencil
- squares of colored construction paper
- glue
- colored pencils, crayons, marking pens, or paint
- scissors

2 Research It

Find out something about the landmark, place, group, person, or activity you have chosen. You can look for information in your school or local library. You can talk to people who have lived in the community for a long time. You can call or write to your local chamber of commerce, too. If you are researching a place, you may be able to visit it. Take notes on the information you find.

Here are some questions you can ask about a landmark, place, or event:

- How long has it been in the community?
- What is it? What does it do?
- Why is it important?

Now you're ready to design your quilt square for your community quilt.

How Am I Doing?

Before you make your community quilt, take a few minutes and ask yourself these questions:

- Have I chosen a landmark, place, person, group, or activity that is important to my community?
- Have I found information about my choice?

3 Design Your Square

Decide what your quilt square will look like. On a sheet of construction paper, draw a picture of the person, group, landmark, place, or activity that you have researched.

Around the edges of the paper, glue on a border of a different colored paper. On your square, write the name of your choice. If you want, add an interesting fact about it. Write your name and age below your drawing or on the border.

Tip Make sure all the squares in your community quilt are the same size. That way, they will easily fit together.

4 Make a Quilt

With your classmates, glue all the quilt squares together. You may want to make several small quilts instead of one large one. Display your quilts on a classroom wall.

Then tell the class what you learned about your community. Answer any questions. Have a quilt party, too! Invite other classes in your school to see your community quilt.

If You Are Using a Computer ...

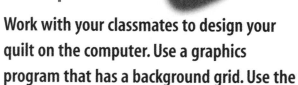

Work with your classmates to design your quilt on the computer. Use a graphics program that has a background grid. Use the Shape Tools to create individual panels. Then type or draw within the squares to show what will go where. Print out your work to use as a guide when you put the quilt together.

JULY 4th
PARADE

Our Mayor
Town Hall
Sam Wada
Age 7
Mayor Jill Lobo

CONGRATULATIONS
You have learned how people improve their communities. What can you do to make your community a better place?

Lorka Muñoz
Community

Glossary

ad•ver•tise•ments
(ad′vər tīz′mənts) *noun*
Public announcements that describe a product or service for sale. TV and radio commercials are advertisements. Advertisements are also found in newspapers and magazines.
▲ **advertisement**

al•pac•a
(al pak′ə) *noun*
An animal that has long silky brown or black wool. An alpaca looks like a llama.

au•di•enc•es
(ô′dē ən səz) *noun*
Groups of people gathered in a place to hear or see something.
▲ **audience**

bulg•ing
(bul′jing) *adjective*
Bursting at the seams or puffed out. That *bulging* suitcase is about to pop open.

bull•doz•er
(bool′dō′zər) *noun*
A tractor with a wide steel blade across the front. It is used to clear land and build roads.

bur•lap (bûr′lap) *noun*
A rough brown cloth. It is used for making bags and other things.

cam•pus
(kam′pəs) *noun*
The grounds and buildings of a school, such as a college.

bulldozer

cha•ran•go
(chə ran′gō) *noun*
An instrument with five strings from South America. A charango looks like a guitar.

crum•pled
(krum′pəld) *verb*
Crushed into a ball.
Karen *crumpled* the
paper in her hand.
▲ **crumple**

dem•on•stra•tion
(dem′ən strā′shən) *noun*
A gathering of many
people in public to
show how they feel
about something. We
held a *demonstration* to
save a playground.

dis•grace
(dis grās′) *noun*
Something that is
shameful. That old
broken-down house is
a *disgrace* to our
neighborhood.

dor•mi•to•ries
(dôr′mi tôr′ēz) *noun*
Places where many
people sleep. ▲ **dormitory**

el•e•men•ta•ry
(el′e men′tə rē) *adjective*
In school, having to do
with kindergarten through
grades four, five, or six.

ex•am•i•na•tions
(ig zam′ə nā′shəns)
noun
Close looks or
inspections.
▲ **examination**

for•eign
(fôr′in) *adjective*
From another country.
We cooked a dinner of
foreign foods.

gar•bage
(gär′bij) *noun*
Scraps of food and other
trash to be thrown away.

har•vest (här′vist) *verb*
To gather a crop when it
is ripe. Farmer Tompkins
will *harvest* her corn in
August.

haze (hāz) *noun*
Fine mist, smoke, or dust
in the air.

In•cas (ing′kəs) *noun*
Members of a Native
American people who
lived in the South
American country of Peru
before the Spanish
takeover in 1535. ▲ **Inca**

in•dus•tri•al
(in dus′trē əl) *adjective*
Having a large number
of businesses or factories.

a	add	͝o͞o	took	ə =
ā	ace	o͞o	pool	a in *above*
â	care	u	up	e in *sicken*
ä	palm	û	burn	i in *possible*
e	end	yo͞o	fuse	o in *melon*
ē	equal	oi	oil	u in *circus*
i	it	ou	pout	
ī	ice	ng	ring	
o	odd	th	thin	
ō	open	ᵺ	this	
ô	order	zh	vision	

Glossary

in•spec•tors
(in spek´tərz) *noun*
People who look over official papers with care. The *inspectors* looked at our passports when we arrived at the airport.
▲ **inspector**

lla•mas (lä´məz) *noun*
Animals from South America related to camels but are smaller and have no humps. Llamas carry heavy loads. Their wool is used for making cloth.
▲ **llama**

Fact File

• When a **llama** gets angry, it spits.
• Llamas have big eyes with long eyelashes that make them look cute.
• Llamas can live at very high places in mountains.

ma•chine
(mə shēn´) *noun*
A tool that has moving parts that work together to do a special job. A lawn mower is a *machine* that cuts grass.

me•di•a
(mē´dē ə) *noun*
All the ways of giving people news and entertainment. Radio, television, newspapers, and magazines are part of the *media*.

mi•grate (mī´grāt) *verb*
To move from one country to another. Many people from other countries *migrate* to America.

mire (mīr) *noun*
An area of muddy, wet, soft ground. After it rained, our car became stuck in the *mire*.

new•com•ers
(noo´kum´ərz) *noun*
People who have recently arrived in a place. Our neighbors in the blue house are *newcomers* from Pakistan.
▲ **newcomer**

par•ti•ci•pate
(pär tis´ə pāt´) *verb*
To be a part of an activity with others; to take part in something.

pe•ti•tion
(pə tish´ən) *noun*
A written statement that asks someone to do something. People who agree with the person making the statement sign the petition.

pro•grams
(prō´gramz) *noun*
Entertainment seen in theaters, on television, or heard on the radio. During the school year, we gave three musical *programs* for our parents.
▲ **program**

pro•tes•ters
(prō´tes tûrz) *noun*
People who speak out against an idea or decision. The *protesters* shouted at the men who want to tear up the town park. ▲ **protester**

re•cit•ed (ri sī´ted) *verb*
Spoke from memory in front of a group. Oscar *recited* some poems for his class. ▲ **recite**

re•pair (ri pâr´) *verb*
To fix something that is broken.

Thesaurus

repair
fix
mend

rub•bish (rub´ish) *noun*
Material to be thrown out; trash.

rust•y (rus´tē) *adjective*
Covered with rust. Rust is a reddish-brown coating that forms on iron or steel when it is wet for too long.

rusty

signs (sīnz) *noun*
Boards or cards covered with writing or pictures that give information.
▲ **sign**

slums (slumz) *noun*
Very poor and crowded areas in a city. ▲ **slum**

smog (smog) *noun*
A mixture of smoke and fog in the air.

Word Study

The word **smog** was made from two other words, *smoke* and *fog*. By putting the first two letters of *smoke* together with the last two letters of fog, you have a new word—**smog**.

smoke•stacks
(smōk´staks´) *noun*
Tall chimneys or pipes that carry smoke away from a factory.
▲ **smokestack**

sup•port•ive
(sə pôr´tiv) *adjective*
Helpful or encouraging. Bill is *supportive* of Mary's idea to change recess hours.

sur•veyed
(sər vād´) *verb*
Asked for information or opinions from a number of people. The store manager *surveyed* his customers to find out whether they liked peas or carrots more.
▲ **survey**

teach•ers
(tē´chərz) *noun*
People who teach in a school or college.
▲ **teacher**

ter•ra•ces
(ter´əs əz) *noun*
Flat areas cut out of hills. People often plant flowers or vegetables on terraces. ▲ **terrace**

a	add	o͝o	took	ə =
ā	ace	o͞o	pool	a in *above*
â	care	u	up	e in *sicken*
ä	palm	û	burn	i in *possible*
e	end	yo͞o	fuse	o in *melon*
ē	equal	oi	oil	u in *circus*
i	it	ou	pout	
ī	ice	ng	ring	
o	odd	th	thin	
ō	open	ŧh	this	
ô	order	zh	vision	

Authors & Illustrators

Arthur Dorros   *pages 106–117*

This author/illustrator's career almost ended when he was in fifth grade. He had always loved to draw, but he often got frustrated with how his pictures came out. In high school, he started drawing again and hasn't stopped! Later he began writing his own books, too. Arthur Dorros spent a year living in South America. This experience led him to write his award-winning book *Tonight Is Carnaval*.

Lisa Campbell Ernst   *pages 82–101*

Lisa Campbell Ernst says, "I have always loved animals, so of course I love to draw them." She notices animals wherever she goes, and many of her books also have animals in them. She was living in New York City when she got the idea for *Squirrel Park*.

Eloise Greenfield   *pages 66–73*

Eloise Greenfield likes to listen to the sound of words. She hopes that her poems and books inspire others to have what she calls "word-madness." She also wants her books to provide "a true knowledge of Black heritage, including both the African and American experiences."

Ellen Levine *pages 56–65*

As a child, Ellen Levine loved to read. "A book could transport me to another time or place," she says. Now Ellen Levine writes books for young readers that transport them to other times and places. She interviewed hundreds of people and read many old journals and letters to collect the information she needed for . . . *If Your Name Was Changed at Ellis Island.*

Arnold Lobel *pages 10–19*

People often asked Arnold Lobel which of his many books was his favorite. He always gave the same answer. "My favorite is always the next one, the one I haven't done yet." Throughout his career as an author and illustrator, he worked on over 70 books. Arnold Lobel died in 1987.

Chris Van Allsburg *pages 22–45*

Chris Van Allsburg says, "The way to get good at something is by doing it a lot." When he was in elementary school, Van Allsburg liked art class so much he would go to school even when he was sick if he had art that day. Drawing was just a hobby for Chris Van Allsburg, until a friend suggested he try to illustrate a book. He's now one of the most popular author/illustrators in America. "I have a favorite kind of mood I like in my art," he says. "I like things to be mysterious."

Books &

Author/Illustrator Study

More by Chris Van Allsburg

Jumanji
A girl and her brother find that a new game leads them to an amazing adventure.

Two Bad Ants
Get an ant's-eye view of an ordinary home in this funny book.

The Wreck of the Zephyr
Something mysterious has happened to a ship, the *Zephyr*, and all of her crew.

Chris Van Allsburg

Fiction

The Best Town in the World
by Byrd Baylor
illustrated by Ronald Himler
Where is the best town in the world? What makes it so special? The boy in this story is sure he knows the answers.

The Village of Round and Square Houses
by Ann Grifalconi
An old African story explains why men live in square houses and women in round ones.

Yagua Days
by Cruz Martel
illustrated by
Jerry Pinkney
What's a yagua day? A New York City boy finds out when he visits his parents' hometown in Puerto Rico.

Nonfiction

Powwow
by George Ancona
What music! What dancing! What fun! Beautiful color photographs help capture the excitement of this Native American celebration.

Recycle! A Handbook for Kids
by Gail Gibbons
Are you part of a recycling project? There are lots of things you can do at home, at school, and in your community to help reuse materials.

The Town That Moved
by Mary Jane Finsand
When iron ore was discovered underneath their town, the people of Hibbing had to move. But they didn't move out of town. They took their town with them. Here is the amazing true story of how they did it.

&Media

 Videos

 Software

Magazines

Videos

The Butter Battle Book
Turner/Good Times
This animated retelling of Dr. Seuss's favorite book is about the best way to eat bread and butter. Because the Yooks and Zooks can't agree, they end up going to war! (30 minutes)

Koi and the Kola Nuts
Rabbit Ears
Koi sets out to find a new village—one where he will be treated as a king's son. Whoopi Goldberg narrates this wise and funny African tale. (30 minutes)

The Lone Star Kid
Public Media
Brian's town is going to elect a new mayor—and eleven-year-old Brian wants the job! This is based on a true story. (58 minutes)

Software

SimCity
Maxis
(Macintosh Plus, IBM)
Where do the roads go? How tall should the buildings be? Design and run a city—all by yourself.

Magazines

3-2-1 Contact
Children's Television Workshop
This science and technology magazine has stories, art, and photos. It includes articles about the environment and how technology helps communities solve problems.

U*S*Kids
Field Publications
Would you like to know more about the world around you? This magazine includes news, true-life stories, and information about the environment.

A Place to Write

Hannah Lindahl Children's Museum
1402 South Main Street
Mishawaka, IN 46454

This museum displays objects that show what life is like in Mishawaka and its sister city in Japan. Write for information about the museum and the sister-cities project.

Acknowledgments

Grateful acknowledgment is made to the following sources for permission to reprint from perviously published material. The publisher has made diligent efforts to trace the ownership of all copyrighted material in this volume and believes that all necessary permissions have been secured. If any errors or omissions have inadvertently been made, proper corrections will gladly be made in future editions.

Cover: Margaret Cusak.

Interior: "On the Day Peter Stuyvesant Sailed Into Town" from ON THE DAY PETER STUYVESANT SAILED INTO TOWN by Arnold Lobel. Copyright © 1971 by Arnold Lobel. Reprinted by permission of HarperCollins Publishers.

"How Pittsburgh Cleaned Up" and cover from SCHOLASTIC ENVIRONMENTAL ATLAS OF THE UNITED STATES by Mark Mattson, map by Christopher Salvatico. Copyright © 1993 by Scholastic Inc. Reprinted by permission.

"Just a Dream" from JUST A DREAM by Chris Van Allsburg. Copyright © 1990 by Chris Van Allsburg. Reprinted by permission of Houghton Mifflin Co. All rights reserved.

"Linden Heights Neighborhood Vegetable Garden" poster from Park District Dayton-Montgomery County's Grow With Your Neighbors Program. Used by permission.

Selections and cover from IF YOUR NAME WAS CHANGED AT ELLIS ISLAND by Ellen Levine, illustrated by Wayne Parmenter. Text copyright © 1993 by Ellen Levine. Illustrations copyright © 1993 by Scholastic Inc. Reprinted by permission of Scholastic Inc.

Selection and cover from MARY McLEOD BETHUNE by Eloise Greenfield, illustrated by Jerry Pinkney. Text copyright © 1977 by Eloise Greenfield. Illustrations copyright © 1977 by Jerry Pinkney. Reprinted by permission of HarperCollins Publishers.

"Family Biscuits" recipe from THE BLACK FAMILY REUNION COOKBOOK, copyright © 1991 by The National Council of Negro Women, Inc. Used by permission of Tradery House, an imprint of The Wimmer Companies, Inc. of Memphis, TN.

"Squirrel Park" from SQUIRREL PARK by Lisa Campbell Ernst. Copyright © 1993 by Lisa Campbell Ernst. This edition is reprinted by arrangement with Simon & Schuster Books for Young Readers, Simon & Schuster Children's Publishing Division.

"Protecting a Park" and cover from KID HEROES OF THE ENVIRONMENT ($4.95) copyright © 1991, by The EarthWorks Group. Cover illustration by Steve Purcell. Published by EarthWorks Press, Berkeley, CA. Used with permission.

"Tonight Is Carnaval" from TONIGHT IS CARNAVAL by Arthur Dorros. Text copyright © 1991 by Arthur Dorros. Illustrations copyright © 1991 by Dutton Children's Books. Used by permission of Dutton Children's Books, a division of Penguin Books USA Inc.

Source logo from "Carnival in the Snow" used by permission of Saint Paul Festival and Heritage Foundation.

Cover from CITY GREEN by DyAnne DiSalvo-Ryan. Illustration copyright © 1994 by DyAnne DiSalvo-Ryan. Published by William Morrow & Company, Inc.

Cover from CLOUDY WITH A CHANCE OF MEATBALLS by Judi Barrett, drawn by Ron Barrett. Drawing copyright © 1978 by Ron Barrett. Published by Atheneum Books for Young Readers, Simon & Schuster Children's Publishing Division.

Cover from LILY AND MISS LIBERTY by Carla Stevens, illustrated by Deborah Kogan Ray. Illustration copyright © 1992 by Deborah Kogan Ray. Published by Scholastic Inc.

Cover from SAMUEL'S CHOICE by Richard Berleth, illustrated by James Watling. Illustration copyright © 1990 by James Watling. Published by Albert Whitman & Company.

Photography and Illustration Credits

Photos: © John Lei for Scholastic Inc. all Tool Box items unless otherwise noted. p. 2 bl: © John Lei for Scholastic Inc.; cl: © John Bessler for Scholastic Inc.; tl: © Dennie Eagleson for Scholastic Inc. pp. 2-3 background: Dennie Eagleson for Scholastic Inc. p. 3 br: © Dennie Eagleson for Scholastic Inc.; tc: © F. Stuart Westmorland/Photo Researchers. p. 4 c: © Francis Clark Westfield for Scholastic Inc.; tc: © F. Stuart Westmorland/Photo Researchers, Inc. p. 5 c: © Ana Esperanza Nance for Scholastic Inc.; tc: © F. Stuart Westmorland/Photo Researchers, Inc. p. 6 c: © Ana Esperanza Nance for Scholastic Inc.; tc: © F. Stuart Westmorland/Photo Researchers, Inc. p. 20 cl, cr: © Carnegie Library of Pittsburgh. p. 46 bl, hand: © Ken Frick for Scholastic Inc.; © F. Stuart Westmorland/Photo Researchers, Inc.; all others: © Lorka Munoz/Wegerzyn Horticultural Center, OH. p. 47 cr: © Leonard Rue III/Photo Researchers, Inc.; all others: © Dennie Eagleson for Scholastic Inc. p. 48 bl: © Dennie Eagleson for Scholastic Inc.; cr: © Lorka Muñoz; bc: © Grant Huntington for Scholastic Inc. p. 49 cr: © Dennie Eagleson for Scholastic Inc.; tc: © David S. Waitz for Scholastic Inc. pp. 50-51 c: © John Lei for Scholastic Inc. p. 52 br: © Stanley Bach for Scholastic Inc.; bl: © Call/West Stock. p. 53 bl, tr: © John Lei for Scholastic Inc. p. 53 br: © Dennis Eagleson for Scholastic Inc. p. 54-55 c: © "Pot Luck" quilt by Cochran. p. 74 cr: © Catherine Baumann for Scholastic Inc. p. 75 bc: © Ed Quinn/NYT Pictures. pp. 76-77 all: © John Lei for Scholastic Inc. p. 78 bc, br: © Stanley Bach for Scholastic Inc. p. 78-79 bc, tc, tr: © John Lei for Scholastic Inc. p. 79 br: © Dennie Eagleson for Scholastic Inc. pp. 80-81 c: © "Homebody" quilt by Sally A. Sellers. pp. 102-103 c: © The Tennessean. pp. 106-117 background: © Richard Megna/Fundamental Photographs for Scholastic Inc. pp. 118-119 c: © Greg Ryan/Sally Beyer/Minnesota Office of Tourism. p. 119 tr: © Wintertainment Foundation of the St. Paul Festival & Heritage Foundation. p. 120 tl: © Ken Karp for Scholastic Inc.; cr: © Richard Megna/ Fundamental Photographs for Scholastic Inc.; br: © Greg Ryan/Sally Beyer. p. 121 tc: © Ken Karp for Scholastic Inc.; cr: © Minnesota Office of Tourism. p. 121 bl: © Greg Ryan/Sally Beyer. pp. 122-123 c: © John Lei for Scholastic Inc. p. 124 br: © Bob Burch/Bruce Coleman, Inc.; bl: © Larry Tackett/Tom Stack & Associates. p. 125 tr: © Sylvain Grandadam/Tony Stone Images; cr: © Stanley Bach for Scholastic Inc. pp. 126-127 c: © Stanley Bach for Scholastic Inc. p. 127 br: © Dennis Eagleson for Scholastic Inc. p. 128 cr: © Derek Redfearn/The Image Bank. p. 131 bc: © Guido Alberto Rossi/The Image Bank. p. 132 tl: © Courtesy of Scholastic Trade Department; cl: © Courtesy of Simon & Schuster. p. 133 tr: © Courtesy of Scholastic Trade Department; cr: © Courtesy of Scholastic Photo Library; br: © Houghton Miffin, Chris Van Allsburg. p. 135 bc: © Porterfield/Chickering/Photo Researchers, Inc.; c: © Patrick Donehue/Photo Researchers, Inc. p. 136 br: © Stephen Ogilvy for Scholastic Inc.

Illustrations: pp. 8-9: Margaret Cusack.